SONGWRITING

HOW TO START A SONG

By Egils Petersons

Copyright © 2015 Egils Petersons

All rights reserved. No part of this book may be reproduced or transmitted in any form or by any means, electronic or mechanical, including photocopying, recording, or by any information storage and retrieval system, without permission in writing from the author.

Join my mailing list to know when
My next book is released!

www.yoursongwriting.com

Table of Contents

Introduction	5
How to Start	7
Inspiration and Creativity	9
Mindset	13
Motivation (How to Stay Motivated)	17
Starting with a Musical Phrase That Comes into Your Mind (It's My Favorite!)	19
Song Structure	22
Contrasts	27
Starting With a Melody	29
Writing a Song on Guitar	31
Starting With a Chord Progression	34
Starting With a Guitar Riff	37
Some Guitar Riff Application Types Could Be:	39
Starting With Lyrics	42
Starting With a Title	47
Writing a Song If You Don't Play Any Instrument	49
Problems	51
Writer's Block	53
How to Freestyle Rap	54
Some Songwriting Tips	57
Conclusion	61

Introduction

Writing songs has sometimes been known for being hard and very complicated to do. Some people get very frustrated and don't have a single clue of what to do after they try to write a song or just a single verse. This happens to a lot of people, because in a way, songwriting is a talent. But the good news is that **we all have the talent**; the difference is that a few work to develop and improve it, and others do not. So all you have to do is improve your skills.

Obviously, no one is born with the talent at its best. All famous songwriters have become recognized, because little by little, they have improved their songwriting skills. How? By **practicing and experimenting until they get what they want.** And everyone can do it as well. You only need some advice and a little help, and you will see that songwriting has suddenly become a whole lot easier for you.

The most important aspect of songwriting is **learning to be patient**. Don't get frustrated and quit too early, because nobody has ever gotten anywhere quitting when things get a little complicated. **Stay focused and be persistent** if you can't write an entire song in just one sitting or, at least, not a great one. You can only get better with time.

"Every child is an artist, with imagination and the artistic instinct. Life stamps these out..." -- Percy Mackaye

We have all heard about how a song should always be written with a certain set of rules, while others claim that they need to be inspired by feelings. What I am going to do here is tell you some great tips that will help you write a song and get rid of that creative block you can experience from time to time.

You feel like having no talent or abilities. Then start with any of the recommended ways, and slowly you will discover your strengths. I believe, if God has put in your heart a desire to write songs, He has also given you an ability to do it.

It is important to use your strengths instead of torturing yourself with things you are not good at doing. Songwriting should be fun!

How to Start

How to Start a Song

As I mentioned, it's very individual. You have to choose the tactic that best suits your talents. Even professional songwriters may experience difficulties starting a new song. However, if you do not know how to implement your ideas into a song, it's not a reason to abandon songwriting. The good news is that you can start very quickly and finish the song in a short time, but you must be ready.

People sometimes do not start writing a song, because they:

1) Think that they do not have enough time at present, so it is better not to begin;

2) Do not feel the inspiration, so they better do something else that is less important for them than songwriting;

3) Have no ideas what to write about.

In reality, all these reasons are usually self-deception. It is a psychological barrier. The real reasons we hesitate can be lack of self-confidence, lack of motivation, wrong mindset, fear of starting something new, and ignorance of how to begin.

In fact, it often happens that a good song comes from nowhere. Start from scratch; start with no matter what. **Start with what you have, and you will be given more.**

SONGWRITING

If you have great difficulties when you start writing a song, and you do not have inspiration and ideas, I can suggest a good way of action. Take a known song and start modifying it: change chords, cut down some of them or modify them, play with the words, change them, giving new meaning to the song, change the melody, and see what comes of it all. You must be careful not to make caricature of the song; it will not make much sense.

When you start the song, don't be a perfectionist; do not criticize it at this point. Don`t be confused if your first song drafts do not look like the next hit song. Think that your task now is not to create a hit song, but to enjoy the process and develop your songwriting skills.

Inspiration and Creativity

Inspiration Comes in Waves

Successful artists are able to gain inspiration from almost anything they hear, feel, or see. Sometimes, the voice of inspiration is very quiet, so make it a habit to listen when any melody begins to sound in your head, as it is easy to miss it. Therefore, you should always carry a notebook or voice recorder with you.

Sometimes, a song can come to you when you're asleep. It is like *Keith Richards* received a guitar riff for the famous *Rolling Stones* song *"Satisfaction"* in a dream. He woke up, grabbed the guitar, recorded it into his recorder, and went back to sleep. *Paul McCartney* received the entire melody of the song *"Yesterday"* in a dream.

And yet, I do not advise to wait for inspiration, but to make songwriting a daily habit- writing at least 15 minutes, without waiting for inspiration. And if it is possible, do it in the morning before all the other minor works - before Facebook, before reading e-mails, etc.

Then inspiration will begin to visit you more often, and it will begin to serve you, rather than you being dependent on it. Write at least 15 minutes, without doing any previous extensive preparation - such as sitting down cozily, etc. Simply, in the circumstances that you are in, do it without waiting for inspiration; take your instrument or voice recorder and start.

Another problem is that inspiration tends to disappear as fast as it emerges. It is therefore advisable to continue and complete at least the main lines of the song, if it's possible, no matter how good or bad it may seem to you, because in such a way, you will develop your songwriting skills, and in my opinion, it is far more important than a particular song.

Therefore, regular work is more important than inspiration. Don't allow your songwriting to depend on inspiration. **Songwriting is a choice ... and action.**

Songwriting is work, the same as the other works, and in order to do it successfully, you need to acquire certain skills. I think the best way to learn them is by writing songs. Sure it is good to attend courses or read a good book, and yet without the active action (writing songs), it will not have any value.

The state of knowledge can be useful to you only when you go through the doubts, difficulties, and inner struggles and find your style and your own way of expression. You will probably have many failures, and maybe, you will write many songs of little value. I've read a lot of information about failures and successes of famous people. *Michael Jordan, Sting, The Beatles, Neil Young* and so on – they all have passed through hard times and failures. In my opinion, all the famous people have gone through failures.

But it is important not to quit. The real failure is when you quit doing something.

So my suggestion is to write as much as possible on a regular basis for at least 15 minutes every day, without waiting for inspiration, and the main thing - *if you really want to be a successful composer - consider the fact that you will write a certain percentage of poor and very unfortunate songs. Initially, the rate may be high.*

> **"Be sure to welcome failure, because then you have no fear!" -Neil Young**

So one of the beginners` main mistakes is that they do not work, but are waiting for inspiration, and when it comes, they are not able to complete the track, and inspiration has already faded away. Then they are waiting for the next time, and the unfinished work is piling up and causing discomfort, procrastination, and the main thing - lack of self-confidence.

There is one more thing that helps me - it is listening to people and what they say. Listen and remember some interesting words and expressions; write them down immediately. I think there are some attractive and interesting people among your friends. If not, you can listen to various speakers and comedians; listen to kids speaking or read an interesting article, read books and jot down interesting thoughts or words you were inspired by.

SONGWRITING

"Doubt can only be removed by action." -Johann Wolfgang von Goethe

Mindset

It sounds like hard work, doesn't it? Sometimes, the problem is that you're tuned to the result, rather than the process. It can deprive you of the joy of creation and convert your songwriting into extremely hard work or torment. Maybe you're influenced by a book or article's title: How to write a hit song, etc... I am not saying that these books are always bad, but they can be useful as a guide if you know how to use them without damaging the joy of the song creation process.

I believe that if you are learning to enjoy your songwriting, then you can become truly productive. And - the key to what you need to focus on during the song creation is **not whether it will appeal to others, but whether you like it yourself**. Do not try to create a hit song. This can shift your focus on pleasing others…

Do not compare yourself with others and do not try to imitate someone. God has created each of us with our unique characteristics and talents and with specific perspective on things. Do not try to create a hit song, instead of expressing yourself, your emotions, and thoughts in the song.

You should develop positive beliefs about you and your music. The first step is to realize that no one on this planet has exactly the same taste of music as you have. You are

unique, and there is something that only you can give to your listeners. Of course, it can fail at once, but with each subsequent song, you will gradually be closer to the main goal - to your style and the ability to express yourself in your songs.

Probably, you've heard many times: *"Be yourself!"* But what does it really mean, and is it always as easy to do as it sounds? In reality, it is also a process that you are learning little by little, always reminding yourself to compose a song, so you like it first. And if you like it, then definitely, it will appeal to someone else.

But if you don't really like your song, then, even if you succeed, your success can be short, and you will not be really pleased and satisfied. So you have to learn to be yourself. It can be a very long process, and you may even experience some failures before you find **your own unique way**. We have senselessly taken into ourselves many ideas about what music and lyrics should be, so it is not so easy to break through the jungle of these assumptions and find our own path.

Think of songwriting as a very pleasant process. **It is an enjoyable process**. However, people often find it to be a very hard struggle, which requires making a great effort. Mostly, it is due to your mindset and fear.

"Whatever course you decide upon, there is always someone to tell you that you are wrong..." -Ralph Waldo Emerson

HOW TO START A SONG

	You Might Think:	You Should Think:
1.	I do not feel sufficiently competent or talented to write a good song.	Many famous songwriters have gone through the doubts of their composer's talent and abilities. If you do not try, you will never know what you are able to.
2.	People that surround me often do not understand me, and I think they will not understand my creative work either.	If you write a song that you like, definitely there will be someone else who will love it. You shouldn't please everyone.
3.	Completely unconsciously, I try to please other people with my song, instead of focusing on it so that I like it.	*You can't please everyone so you gotta please yourself. - Ricky Nelson.*
4.	Good song must comply with many different laws that I do not know.	Many prominent songwriters have not studied music at all.
5.	Songwriting is very hard work.	Songwriting is a very enjoyable process. It is freedom to express yourself in a way you like.
6.	I currently do not have much time, and I do not feel inspired to write right now.	There'll never be a perfect time. Take a few minutes to write a couple of sentences, musical phrases, etc.

When you are composing a song, you're doing something over which you have full and unlimited power. You have absolute freedom to write your song as you wish it to be. This awareness can give wings to your creativity and bring interesting results. Enjoy this freedom! You don't have to copy anyone, and you don't have to use clichés; you can speak in your own words.

Above all, you should enjoy it, and even if you find out you are no *Mozart* or *Lennon & McCartney*, there is something very satisfying about transmuting some bit of yourself into a set of sounds.

Practice makes perfect

Write songs every day. Believe that practice makes perfect. When you write every day, your writing skills gradually get better. This is one of the most obvious, yet effective, songwriting tips. Keep writing without giving any verdict about the output, no matter how bad the writing. If you are gadget savvy, you can record your ideas with a recorder for later reference. You should better develop this as a habit. You will realize how advantageous it is. Perhaps you will not end up with a complete song within a day. But even a few lines are constructive. So keep writing!

> *"Don't judge each day by the harvest you reap, but by the seeds that you plant." -Robert Louis Stevenson*

Motivation (How to Stay Motivated)

In my opinion, the main motivating element should be - enjoying the songwriting process in itself- to find interest and pleasure in the process of creation.

There are many different things that motivate people to write songs. These can be deadlines, competition with others (competition between *Lennon* and *McCartney*), chances of success, money, other people's appreciation etc. Also there can be the total opposite of motivators – enjoying the process of songwriting, expressing themselves, creation of music purely for fun and relaxation.

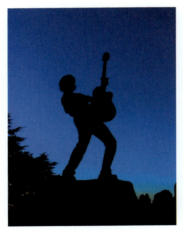

You should experience the pleasure and joy from the songwriting process. I'm a guitarist, and at some stage, I tried to set a goal for myself: every day 3 hours of playing exercises. But for me, it was not working. I was annoyed, because it was incredibly boring. People are different. For some, it certainly works, but not for me. When I found my own way to practice playing the guitar, then I was able to spend a lot of time with the guitar and feel the joy, and the time flew by unnoticed.

I used to turn on the TV or play some CDs and improvise along with what sound, all the time trying to stay in

SONGWRITING

harmony and tonality that unexpectedly changed. For me, it was interesting; **it was a game**. Also, you have to find your own unique approach to songwriting, the one that you are having fun, instead of torture. I heard an interview, as *Freddie Mercury* said, if he fails within 15 minutes of a musical theme to create something interesting, then he is eliminated. Everyone has their own approach.

You should feel comfortable with your songwriting. I think it's good not to push yourself. Do not to stress that your song is maybe not good enough. It is a very special feeling to write a new song, especially if you have already had an idea in your mind for some time. However, many people find it quite a difficult task to get a song out of their mind and onto paper. In particular, the difficulty is in making your musical ideas accessible, visible to others. Unfortunately, many people are abandoning their idea of writing songs, because they do not feel sufficiently talented, or their song does not seem good enough to show to others.

Of course, you can make good money with songwriting. But, try not to consider money as the main stimulation for your writing. If you focus on money mainly, chances of getting discouraged when you fail are higher. Just focus on the subject and keep writing. A good output will automatically make you successful financially.

Starting with a Musical Phrase That Comes into Your Mind (It's My Favorite!)

Be Calm and Let the Song Come to You

"Starting a song is not something that can be forced or come into being because of necessity; most often, it is a relaxed state of mind that allows your creativity to flow. You should avoid creativity-killing thoughts, such as starting with the title to the song, the key, or the structure as that will take you out of the creative process."

From my article (Egils Petersons)

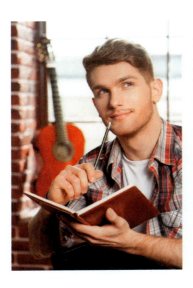

Sometimes, you can hear music, motifs or melodies in your mind. Use them; don't let them disappear! The more you make use of them, the more new melodies you will get. Don't be skeptical, even if those melodies or phrases seem not to be very exciting. Listen to the famous hits; they often start with a very plain and simple motif, but later develop into a hit.

There are people who, occasionally, get some unheard musical motifs in their minds. They might not sound very superb or exciting, but it is important that they are original

SONGWRITING

and unheard. I absolutely recommend using those motifs and writing songs.

I noticed that if I use musical motifs coming into my mind, I receive them more and more. If I don't use them, I receive them less and less. So, it's a matter of training or something like that, because sometimes, those motifs are so quiet and almost unnoticeable that I simply miss them. Have you ever noticed that you start humming something to yourself, but it is not anything familiar? It is a musical motif that has visited you.

Paul McCartney spent half a day walking around, inquiring of his friends about the melody: whether it was a known song or if it had come to him from above. It was the melody of the song, *"Yesterday."*

When a musical phrase or melody appears in my head, I don't judge it- is it good or bad. It's very important not to judge it at this stage! Because it's worthless – I don't know – maybe it can develop into a good song or maybe not. Pull out one musical phrase of the song that you like, and it is very likely that one phrase in itself will be nothing special.

So I take my guitar, sing my phrase, and try to find my first chord - it can be major or parallel minor or simply 5th. I sing my phrase many times and, if it's possible, use some words (not pushing to that, it is not important for me at this stage). Singing along my phrase many times, I try to add some other chords and find the best result (best for my taste). I try not to push further to develop the melody. Instead, I wait for the next part of the melody to come by

HOW TO START A SONG

itself. Then, in the process, somehow, I start feeling if it's a verse or chorus.

If it's a chorus, I try to make it better and add some words to find the main phrase or sentence of the chorus. I start to understand approximately what this song will be about. The chorus should be bright and expressive, and it should contain the main idea of the song, which sometimes, is the same as the title. When I've got that feeling that the chorus is good, I start thinking about verses. The verse should be much simpler than the chorus. This consecution is not always the same; it may vary of course. It's only one example.

Song Structure

In songwriting, you do not necessarily need a degree in order to compose a great song, but you have to **learn the basics**. Know the difference between harmony and melody, and also learn the basic chords and notes.

Analyzing Other People's Songs

When you are planning to write a song, you may want to listen to great artists and musicians first. A good listener can easily become a good songwriter. Make it a habit to listen to hit songs and try to follow their pattern. It does not mean that you should put your ideas away at all. Listening to hit songs will allow you to understand the secret formula behind them.

Listen to the **melody** and **lyrics** then study the possible structures. When you write a song, you need to pay special attention to the **form** and **structure**. If you analyze the proper structure and form, you will not have to go through much hassle when writing a song. The most common or standard song structure is composed of **intro**, **verse**, **chorus**, another **verse,** then followed by a **bridge** and will end with a chorus repeated once or more. Check how verses were written; these are important, since they are where the stories are told.

Intro

Basically, the introduction appears at the start of the song. You might have noticed in popular music that it ideally lasts between four to eight bars. For other music genres, like dance and rock, this rule is not usually applied. The main function of the introduction is to catch the attention of the listeners. It must pull the listeners in order to make them want to hear the other parts of the song. The intro is usually instrumental.

Verse

Since every song has its own story to convey, the aim of the verse is to tell the story. The melody of the verse would be the same each time. However, when it comes to the lyrical aspect, the verse differs as each develops the story. Ideally, verses are slightly quieter compared to the chorus.

Pre-Chorus

This appears between the verse and the chorus. The purpose of the pre-chorus is to place an additional layer of dynamics to the song. It is usually added in order to create tension up to the song's chorus. This is usually between two to eight bars.

Chorus

There is no denying the fact that the chorus is the most essential part of a song. It is a section that will be repeated after each verse and in which the author or the singer can convey the message of the song. A chorus is said to be great when it is **memorable** and **catchy**. Listeners will remember the chorus even better if it includes the "hook" or title of the song.

Bridge

This part of the song usually comes after the secondary chorus with the goal to add contrast. The bridge can either be an instrumental solo, a new chord progression, a new lyrical message, or the like. It usually lasts no longer than eight bars.

Outro

Outro is used to denote the end part of the song. This is usually the part when the story fades out. It can also be in the form of a chorus, which is repeated a couple of times, while the singer uses ad lib.

Hooks

It is important to create catchy tones and tunes, but never forget to write the **hooks,** or the most interesting and captivating lines in a song. People remember the tune and also some words and lines that are not common, surprising, or funny. It makes people sing the song over and over, even unintentionally, because it remains in their minds.

The lyrics of your song should have a meaning, and your fans will grab the message in it. If you can deliver a powerful message through lyrics, you have a higher chance of making your song a popular one. This message is supposed **to be heard** by another person. Therefore, it is recommended to write it in **simple language** so that anyone can understand.

HOW TO START A SONG

The lyrics of your song should **match** perfectly well with the melody, or else, it will become a prose or a poem. The melody plays an important role in connecting music with words. In other words, the melody of your song will resemble the words that are in your song.

Usually, a song starts with a concept or an idea. There are some writers who start with the melody and then add words accordingly. On the other hand, you can find songwriters who start with words and create a suitable melody. It is up to you to select the perfect method out of these two. **There is not a wrong way or right way** to write your song. If you pay attention to the above mentioned tips, you will be able to write a good song.

The next song structure I give you is optional. There can be songs without intro, solo, bridge, or without chorus. It's totally up to you.

SONGWRITING

	INTRO	Short And Attractive INSTRUMENTAL Part It can be a guitar riff (or other instrument) or the part of the chorus without singing
A	VERSE 1 VERSE 2	Tell your story! (SINGING) VERSES - the same melody, different lyrics. Not too much backing, it repeats a few times before moving on to the chorus
	PRE-CHORUS (optional)	Channel between verse and chorus (SHORT), builds the song up, dynamics get louder, texture gets thicker
B	CHORUS	The CATCHY PART Of The Song (Main idea) CHORUSES - the same melody, the same lyrics. Include your title in the chorus (optional)! Fuller instrumentation, maybe louder than verse.
	INTRO (optional)	Intro riff (optional)
A	VERSE 3 (VERSE 4)	The same Verse's melody, different lyrics.
	PRE-CHORUS	(Optional)
B	CHORUS	The same CHORUS as first. The new backup, vocal, the thickest section
	INSTRUMEN-TAL SOLO (optional)	Guitar, keyboard or any other instrument solo.
C	BRIDGE	A part that contrasts with the verse. Something different from verse and chorus. Do something new here in a new key!
B	CHORUS	You can repeat chorus two or three times
	OUTRO	Intro riff (optional)

26

Contrasts

Make your songs very dynamic. Make them peak and subside, instead of staying on the same level the whole song. This will make your song interesting and unpredictable. It is good to create contrasts **between the parts of the song**. Some common types of contrasts could be different instrument sounds of verse and chorus, rhythmic contrasts, and melodic and harmonic contrasts.

A good example of harmonic contrast between verse and chorus is *Mixed Emotions by The Rolling Stones*. All the verse is built on one chord D, and it contrasts well with the nice harmony (chord progression) of the chorus and interesting upward bass line, Am G/B C D. I love it!

If your song starts with a bright, interesting riff, then you should avoid making the 1st verse very melodic and harmonically rich. Very often, after the good guitar riff, there is simple melody based on one or two chords, for example, *Satisfaction (Rolling Stones), Smoke on the water (Deep Purple),* and *Whole Lotta Love (Led Zeppelin).*

Also, don't try to put all your creativity in the 1st verse. Sometimes, the verse is very simple, but it prepares bright choruses, and such contrasts are good for the song. If the song does not have any contrasts, it can become boring.

Listen to different types or genres of music. Yes, you may be interested in a specific genre, and you want to be famous for that kind of song, but there is nothing wrong with opening your mind to more ideas. Great musicians try

SONGWRITING

to incorporate other genres into their crafts and even do experimentations to create unique music for different listeners. When you listen to more kinds of music, you will learn a lot of techniques and styles that may influence you in your songwriting activity.

Starting With a Melody

How to write a melody?

You can pay a teacher to teach you to write a melody. Then, he will start playing or singing a new melody. But you know: **it will be teacher's melody, not yours**. You still won't know how it was created. Ok, the teacher can explain to you that a melody starts at some point, then goes up, then goes down, it moves through notes of one chord, and after, it moves through notes of the other chord. Then, the melody will reach some culmination point, and so on....

But, let me give you an example. Imagine that you are sitting at the table, and there is an apple on the table. There is also your teacher, who then tells you how to take this apple. He will start to explain to you that you must use some muscles of your arm to lift it and some other muscles to stretch it towards an apple. After that, you must use some other muscles to open your palm and then to grab an apple.

But it will be too complicated and too slow and will bring you great confusion. There is another way-**by trying**-and it could be much quicker.

You can choose one or two chords and start playing, humming, and searching for a melody. Then try to find the next chord and the next one-those best suited to your melody and to your own taste. The very first tip is to ensure that you do not rush over this task. It is extremely vital that you take your time and allow the inspiration to come.

SONGWRITING

Try to follow your intuition, listen to yourself, do not hurry, and wait until the feeling comes that this is the right tune. You are humming but do not try to push. I'm not saying this will work for anyone, but I know there are people who will succeed in such a way and who can master it. And it's a great feeling to write a song in this way.

I apply this method not only in songwriting, but also in improvising and playing solos on the guitar. It is the feeling when **you partially lead your improvisation, and it partially leads you**. Such an approach also helps to avoid clichés.

The process of creating a song shouldn't be forced by necessity. The relaxed state of mind and allowing your creativity to flow would give you much better results.

"Experience is the best teacher." - Late 16th; Tacitus

Writing a Song on Guitar

In order to write or compose a song on guitar, it is necessary to learn the **basic chords** first. Some beginners use the most common keys, which are G, D and C. As you learn the other keys, including the sharp keys, you will be able to explore and experiment in songwriting with a guitar.

If you already know the chords, keep on strumming until you create a good sound for the verse, chorus, and bridge. **Strum as if you are just playing** with different chords when you still do not have lyrics. You can try other song structures if you wish to sound unique from other compositions. It does not matter if you start making the melody first, before the lyrics, or the other way around.

Start humming the tune that you like and **sing the verse,** if possible, so you can check if it fits the chords. Play the melody, write the chords or tab it out. It is normal to have difficulty singing while playing during the first rehearsals, so if there is someone who can help you out and sing the song for you, then it would be nice.

People like to hear **unique sounds** and more catchy tunes. That is why you should avoid writing songs with the same keys and chords all the time. Find out which sound is perfect for the style of song that you wish to create. If you cannot avoid using the same keys over and over, then choose a different tempo and pitch to make it sound fresh and new.

SONGWRITING

Common Major Scale Chords in a Corresponding Key

KEY	I	II	III	IV	V	VI	*bVII
C	C	Dm	Em	F	G	Am	Bb
Db	Db	Ebm	Fm	Gb	Ab	Bbm	Cb
D	D	Em	F#m	G	A	Bm	C
Eb	Eb	Fm	Gm	Ab	Bb	Cm	Db
E	E	F#m	G#m	A	B	C#m	D
F	F	Gm	Am	Bb	C	Dm	Eb
Gb	Gb	Abm	Bbm	Cb	Db	Ebm	Fb
G	G	Am	Bm	C	D	Em	F
Ab	Ab	Bbm	Cm	Db	Eb	Fm	Gb
A	A	Bm	C#m	D	E	F#m	G
Bb	Bb	Cm	Dm	Eb	F	Gm	Ab
B	B	C#m	D#m	E	F#	G#m	A

* I added bVII degree, instead of VII, because it is widely used in pop/rock music. For example: *A Hard Day's Night by The Beatles* (G-C-G-F-G, I-IV-I- bVII-I), *All Right Now by Free* (chorus) (A-G-D-A, I- bVII-IV-I), *Crazy Little Thing Called Love by Queen* (D-G-C-G, I-IV-bVII-IV).

HOW TO START A SONG

Common Minor Scale Chords in a Corresponding Key

KEY	I	III	IV	V	V	VI	VII
Cm	Cm	Eb	Fm	Gm	G, G7	Ab	Bb
C#m	C#m	E	F#m	G#m	G#, G#7	A	B
Dm	Dm	F	Gm	Am	A, A7	Bb	C
D#m	D#m	F#	G#m	A#m	A#, A#7	B	C#
Em	Em	G	Am	Bm	B, B7	C	D
Fm	Fm	Ab	Bbm	Cm	C, C7	Db	Eb
F#m	F#m	A	Bm	C#m	C#, C#7	D	E
Gm	Gm	Bb	Cm	Dm	D, D7	Eb	F
G#m	G#m	B	C#m	D#m	D#, D#7	E	F#
Am	Am	C	Dm	Em	E, E7	F	G
Bbm	Bbm	Db	Ebm	Fm	F, F7	Gb	Ab
Bm	Bm	D	Em	F#m	F#, F#7	G	A

Starting With a Chord Progression

If you have a talent to create interesting chord progressions on a keyboard or a guitar, start with them, play with them, and add some words, humming a melody. I think, most likely, the chord progression is not chosen before, but it comes during the process of songwriting. But if you feel like you don't have any good ideas, just come up with a good chord progression, and once you have it, hum a melody as you play the progression. This is going to give you a good start that you can use as a base.

You should also consider the kind of tune you are creating. If it evokes romantic feelings, you should create a song about love, but if it has an aggressive and upbeat sound, you should come up with energetic lyrics that might be about protest or raising awareness. When you have a nice chord progression, you can also try to create a simple solo over it.

HOW TO START A SONG

Some of the Most Often Used Chord Progressions:

I - VI - IV - V	Song	Performed by
A F#m D E	Stand By Me	Ben E. King
F Dm Bb C	Complicated	Avril Lavigne
Db Bbm Gb Ab	Lucky (chorus)	Britney Spears
C Am F G	How Great is Our God (chorus)	Chris Tomlin
B G#m E F#	Wonderful World	Sam Cooke
Ab Fm Db Eb	Every Breath You Take	The Police
A F#m D E	I Will Always Love You	Whitney Houston

I - V - IV - V	Song	Performed by
Db Ab Gb Ab	Everything I Do	Bryan Adams
G D C D	Tangerine (chorus)	Led Zeppelin
D A G A	Under Pressure	Queen
A E D E	You Don't Know What Love Is	The White Stripes
C G F G	All The Small Things	Blink 182
E b Bb Ab Bb	With You	Chris Brown

SONGWRITING

I - VII - VI			Song	Performed by
C#	B	A	Gimme Shelter	Rolling Stones
Cm	Bb	Ab	All Along the Watchtower	Jimi Hendrix
Am	G	F	outro section of Stairway to Heaven	Led Zeppelin
F#m	E	D	Under My Thumb	Rolling Stones

I - V - VI - IV				Song	Performed by
A	E	F#m	D	Someone Like You (chorus)	Adele
A	E	F#m	D	Already Gone	Kelly Clarkson
A	E	F#m	D	The Edge Of Glory (chorus)	Lady Gaga
Ab	Eb	Fm	Db	Paparazzi (chorus)	Lady Gaga
D	A	Bm	G	Girlfriend (chorus)	Avril Lavigne
B	F#	G#m	E	I'm Yours	Jason Mraz

VI - IV - I - V				Song	Performed by
Cm	Ab	Eb	Bb	So Small	Carrie Underwood
Am	F	C	G	Parachute	Cheryl Cole

Starting With a Guitar Riff

A memorable riff can make all the difference

We have all heard songs that are driven by their lyrical power, but there are also many compositions that shine because of their guitar riffs. A good example of a song that has a memorable riff is *Enter Sandman by Metallica* or *Smoke on the Water by Deep Purple*. The point is that a great riff can make a song shine, and the lyrics can be a perfect way to complement a great song structure.

Creating a good riff

A good riff is (not usually, but can be) the product of trial and error during a jam-session. This means, you might be playing some random ideas, and then something seems to click. Once you have an idea you like, you should start working on it and polishing it until you have a riff that you like. This is the way that most great riffs are made. Going back to the *Enter Sandman* example, the band tells a story about how the original riff was created by Kirk, but if it wasn't for the tweaks that Lars added to it, the riff would probably not have been as good, or maybe it could have been even better if they left it as it was.

SONGWRITING

The important thing to take out of that little story about how that riff was made is that you will usually modify a riff at least a little. That is not to say that some riffs have not been composed in a sudden creative moment and have been left exactly as they first came out. Such is the case with *Megadeth's Symphony of Destruction* main riff.

How do you write a song around a riff?

I think it is relatively easy for guitarists to create a good riff, but the main problem for many musicians could be this: ***What's next? How do you write a song around a riff?*** That's why **I tried to analyze** some of excellent songs with good riffs.

Some Guitar Riff Application Types Could Be:

The song starts with a great, memorable riff

The song starts with a great riff then the 1st verse follows at the same key as the riff. Melody is very **static, simple, monotonous**, and sometimes, improvising (the singer improvises a melody), based on one, maybe 2 chords.

Examples:

Deep Purple - Smoke on the Water (verse-2chords G and F),

The Rolling Stones - (I Can't Get No) Satisfaction (verse – 2chords E, A),

Black Sabbath - Paranoid,

Nirvana - Smells Like Teen Spirit.

Riff based songs (the riff continuous during the verse)

Examples:

Cream - Sunshine of Your Love,

Led Zeppelin - Whole Lotta Love,

Red Hot Chili Peppers - Can't stop,

SONGWRITING

Blur - Song 2,

David Bowie - Rebel Rebel (2 chords D and E),

Muse - Supermassive Black Hole (verse-1 chord E),

The White Stripes - Seven Nation Army,

Dire Straits - Money for Nothing,

 AC/DC - Back in Black,

The Beatles - I Feel Fine,

Megadeth - Symphony of Destruction.

You can see in the song, *Can't Stop by Red Hot Chili Peppers,* the riff is continuous during the first verse, and the melody is very monotonous, but the **chorus is contrasting, melodic.**

Riffs based on blues progressions

Examples:

Chuck Berry - Johnny B Goode,

The Kinks - You Really Got Me,

The Beatles -I Feel Fine,

Good Golly Miss Molly-performed by CCR.

Riffs followed by melodic verse

Examples:

Pretty Woman – Roy Orbison

If you have a good riff that is very catchy, then my suggestion would be - the melody of the 1st verse after that riff should be very **static** with one, maybe 2 chords, not more.

Writing a song on guitar should always be an experience that understands the structure of a good song, but is not afraid of exploring ideas. This is going to be the most honest way for anyone to create music. Always follow your instincts and think about how good a song really sounds to you. ***Is the chorus catchy, and are the riffs really good, or just OK?*** These are the kinds of questions you need to ask yourself when writing a song on guitar.

Starting With Lyrics

How to Write Song Lyrics

When it comes to writing melodies and the structure for songs, many musicians have little difficulty expressing the music side of their talent. However, when it comes to how to write song lyrics, it can seemingly be a different matter. In fact, there are many musicians who believe that the art of songwriting cannot be taught, but instead, the person must have that talent already inside them.

This is because the personal expression of music and the lyrics come from two different parts of the brain that must be united in order to create a song. While some may say it takes talent that is already present, there are too many people who have demonstrated the ability to learn how to write lyrics over the years. So, it is not so much inherited talent as understanding how to merge the melody with the words and create a good, solid song.

Where Do Song Lyrics Come From?

There is no end to the sources from where song lyrics may come, but for the most part, they do evolve out of the experiences of the person who is writing the music.

HOW TO START A SONG

Quite often, this is combined with their emotions, feelings, and beliefs that find expression along with the melody. While seemingly profound in concept, some of the most famous song lyrics actually have rather humble origins.

For example, the *Dire Straits'* classic *"Skateaway"* sprang from a taxi cab ride that band leader, *Mark Knopfler*, was taking in London, when he spotted a girl skating down the sidewalk in brightly colored clothing and wearing a brand new Sony Walkman radio. The image that *Knopfler* had was so strong that he constructed the entire melody and lyrics out of the five or ten seconds that he observed the girl.

When it comes to your lyrics, finding the right ones will often come from some type of experience you had, even if it was only dreamed or perhaps imagined. The key is finding the right way to incorporate them into the song itself.

How to Incorporate Lyrics into Songs

So, when you have created the perfect melody, how can you write song lyrics that compliment what you have accomplished? Quite often, the answer does not spring to mind, although there have been exceptions. *Robert Plant* wrote the lyrics to *"Stairway to Heaven"* in just a few minutes, as the inspiration came to him rather quickly.

Unfortunately, the rule, generally, is that you will have to work a little harder than Robert did on that particular song in order to come up with some good lyrics. However, you can emulate what *Robert Plant, Mark Knopfler*, and many other songwriters have done, trying to meld the feelings that you have into words that add to the melody. The only important result is the final one, where you understand what you want out of the words you create for the song.

Hooks: You may have created melodic hooks to your song, but lyrics can provide hooks as well. There are many examples where a certain phrase becomes a hook in the song that compliments the melody and creates a more memorable result in totality. A real plus to creating lyrical hooks is they do not need to be sophisticated to be memorable.

Cher's "Believe" was auto-tuned in certain parts to create a very memorable effect. You can also cite the *Gnarls Barkley* classic, *"Crazy"*, as a song that took a very common word, in fact a word that worked for Patsy Cline's version over a half century ago, and gave it a new meaning. Creating hooks with lyrics is nothing new, but it is something that works out quite well.

Percussive: Another way you can write lyrics for a song is by incorporating the percussive nature of the words themselves. Many rap and hip hop songs use this technique, but it can be used for many different genres. *The Psychedelic Furs*, for example, wrote a song called *"Pulse"* for their first album, which used the words as percussive instruments, where the sound was more important than the meaning of the words themselves.

Message: This may be the most common way to provide a hook for your lyrics in that they convey a message that the audience will understand. This is true, even if the lyrics make no sense. For example, when asked by the producer of their first feature film to write a title song, *Paul McCartney* and *John Lennon* managed to write, *"A Hard Day's Night"* all in one night, built around a throwaway line that *Ringo Starr* had said a few months earlier.

Sourcing Your Lyrics

Whether you choose to create lyrics with hooks, messages, or as percussive instruments, you will need to find the inspiration necessary to create them. The good news is, when it comes to learning how to write song lyrics, the inspiration can come from anywhere. From books, television shows, the radio, the internet, watching people walk across the street or listening to someone say how tough their night was by proclaiming they had to work all day.

It helps if you can combine the feeling the melody gives you with an experience that you had or something you have seen or heard. Quite often, lyrics have inspirations that come from the most unlikely sources, but you have to be aware of the moment when it strikes. This means having a pen and paper handy or perhaps a smartphone in which you can quickly type a message to yourself when the lyrics start to flow.

The initial stages are the most important, as you can then work off of your inspiration and come up with additional lyrics based on your original idea. Of course,

SONGWRITING

you might find that your lyrics will change radically over time, but that is okay, as long as you start the creative process. After all, there is no one way to learn how to write song lyrics, but you can find yourself tapping into a source that provides what is needed to complete the song itself.

Starting With a Title

Some songwriters start their music with a title. The title will be the general topic and their basis for the lines used in the verses and chorus. These songwriters consider the title very important in every aspect of song composition, because all the ideas may come from it. They can list several titles to choose from or simply make a final title in a snap. However, other musicians can just decide about the title afterwards, since they can base it from the lyrics.

The title should be **catchy and easy to remember**. Shorter titles have greater impact, but sometimes meaningful or intriguing, long phrase titles are interesting too. Some musicians do not use direct or clear titles; they use hidden meanings to make the song look mysterious.

It's not for my taste to start a song with a title, but as I mentioned earlier, there is no right or wrong way. You can choose an interesting, catchy title and then build a song around it. **One of the simplest methods is to answer the questions.**

SONGWRITING

For example:

1) I Can't Forgive Her.
   Ask the questions! Why? When did it start? Where did it start? What will be next? What is important to you? What is important to her? Do you know her well? Does she know you? Do you trust her? What should I do? Must I forgive or not? And so on...

2) Millions of Stars.
   Which of them is yours? Which is mine? How did they arise? When did they arise? How long will they shine? What will happen with them? What will happen with us? What will happen with our feelings?

3) My friend.
   What is my friend like? Will he ever gossip about me? Will he be able to forgive? Will he believe me when any other will not? Is love a choice or a feeling?

4) Step By Step
   Do we run? Do we walk? Do we drive? Do we float along with stream of life? What is our direction? What are our goals? What can stop us? Are we directed by fear or by the call of our heart?

Writing a Song If You Don't Play Any Instrument

It is not impossible to write songs, even if you cannot play any musical instrument. Some people have the talent to write lyrics or make a melody even if they cannot read notes or understand chords; these people find themselves **humming** or **whistling** a tune and automatically create a catchy song.

Knowledge in any musical instrument is definitely an advantage for musicians and composers. Nowadays, modern gadgets and apps are available to help any aspiring musician to write or compose a song without playing an instrument.

The most recommended tool in writing a song is the **pre-recorded music tracks** that you can buy from specific websites. There are free options for those who prefer more practical recording. These song tracks are not limited to one genre and are available with a full band setup if needed.

Some websites allow users to record voice, and they **add back up instruments or beats** for free, but if you want to convert the song into MP3 file format, then you have to pay for it, albeit a minimum fee. These websites are fun to use and can give an idea on what tunes and style to use in your composition.

Some aspiring musicians, who cannot play any musical instrument, may not feel comfortable using online recording apps. The best way is to record it just like the **old**

SONGWRITING

way. Get a voice recorder or use your mobile phone recorder then hum the tune if lyrics are not yet available.

When you're done with the melody, lyrics, and song structure, maybe you can **hire someone** to plot your song to chords or tabs. When you have chords and notes, it is easier to ask someone, like another musician or a band mate, to play your song, since they can follow the exact tones that you have created.

When you are planning to write a song, you may want to listen to great artists and musicians first. Listen to the **melody** and **lyrics** then study the possible **structures**. Some songs have long introductions, either instrumental or with lyrics. Check how verses were written; these are important, since these are where the stories are told.

Problems

One of the problems or, rather, features of songwriting can be that while the song is being written, **you do not see it as a whole**. You only see the beginning or the part of the song on which you are working. It is like walking in darkness without seeing where to go.

You may feel that a part on which you are working is still not good, and you modify it; you change it, even though, in the context of the song, it would be good. One of the main mistakes is to try to put **too much** material and ingenuity in the first verse and try to create it to be very impressive. And then there is no longer space for further development and contrasts.

Imagine you walk along one of New York's streets in rush hour, and people are coming towards you, rushing past you, crossing your path. But you continue moving forward, although you can't predict everything in your path trajectory. You do not wait until the street becomes empty, and you will be able to see all your way.

Similarly, when you are composing a song, do not sit at one of its parts, constantly trying to improve it. Go ahead

SONGWRITING

with other parts, and when your song's structure becomes mainly clear, then you can go back and change and improve it.

Writer's Block

I think it is very individual, and everybody has his own approach, but personally, I sometimes feel inspired when I hear a bad song. I have the desire then to write something much better.

The flow of words from brain to paper is a consistently regular task for writers all over the world, and this firmly includes songwriters. However, as you keep writing, there comes that disruptive element that seems to make you feel like you can't go any further, and you need to stop. Now, it's vital to know that it's actually all happening in your mind, when it seems like you can't go further, and you can't think of anything else. Therefore, there are quite a number of ways for songwriters to overcome the song writing block.

The very first thing you need to do is **take a break**. This is the time when you should just walk away and relieve yourself of some of the labour that comes with writing. The important thing to note is that the human brain will always need rest at some point, and due to the level of creativity involved in writing, it is only right that you should give your brain some rest.

If you want to get more tips on writer's block, you can download my FREE report, "15 Tips to Overcome Songwriter's Block", at my site: yoursongwriting.com.

How to Freestyle Rap

I'm not a rap freestyle specialist, but the reason I mentioned it in my book is that, in my opinion, for every songwriter, no matter what style he writes, it would be useful to learn to freestyle rap, because it can improve his lyrics writing skills and elevate them to a new level, as well as improve the ability to improvise.

If you want to learn different techniques, you may listen to other professional rappers who have made albums, singles, or are even known for **freestyle rapping battles**. You may find videos of international artists on the internet and listen to how they deliver the words and notice the rhymes at the end of each line.

There are so many American rappers, who can inspire anyone who wishes to learn the skill in freestyle rapping, such as the late Tupac Shakur and Notorious B.I.G or Eminem. They are known for rap songs with deep meaning. Eminem is more famous for freestyle rapping, since he started joining street battles before he became famous.

Just like any other rapper, you must **listen carefully to the beat** and try to understand the counts in order to fill in the appropriate number of words and syllables. Since you

HOW TO START A SONG

are just a beginner, you may write down your rap lyrics first then look for a simple and average tempo beat on some websites such as *YouTube*.

There are available **videos** with instrumental music or beats, especially made for rappers and enthusiasts, by some DJs. If you have a keyboard instrument at home, you can use the available beats there and adjust the tempo to whatever speed you prefer. Another option is to get a karaoke version of your favorite rap songs and try to compose your own lyrics on the spot.

Do not be disappointed if you cannot follow the beat or cannot think of rhyming words at times, because that happens to everyone, especially to beginners, and that is the reason you have to rehearse often.

Practice **improvising lyrics**. Think of a specific subject, such as Love, War, or Freedom, and think of how you want to describe the topic. Let your mind flow freely and do not force yourself to concentrate on a specific idea.

It is also advisable to **write down rhymes** to the words that you commonly use on your rap pieces. By this, you can create sentences or lines more easily. If you want to focus, you must rehearse in a private area, so you will not be distracted by any other sound, aside from the beat that you are following.

Freestyle rapping includes **fillers**. It is possible for rappers, even the professional ones, to forget the next line or go blank for seconds. The best way to avoid these moments is to use fillers or filler words and phrases, such

SONGWRITING

as yeah, come on, that's right, yo, yes, here it goes. The purpose of fillers is to keep the freestyle rap from falling apart, so it should not be overused, or else, you will end up with a non-sense and boring rap song.

You can be creative and choose funny words or lines, catchy statements and similes, or start your rap lyrics with a shocking intro, but not necessarily something explicit. It is important to feel confident and let your ideas flow and to play with words, as long as it makes a lot of sense and is entertaining.

Some Songwriting Tips

A good song can be created by anyone, even those who may have little to no formal musical training. This is because everyone has an inherent musical ability, and writing a good song does not need tremendous talent to make it happen. However, it does require a little thought, discipline, and ability to translate what is in your head to the page, so your song can become a reality.

Fortunately, there are methods that can make this happen, which songwriters have been using for many decades. By following these tips, you can understand how to make a song a reality.

Tap into Your Emotions

A good song stirs your emotions, so it's no surprise that songwriters will tap into their emotions when writing a song and, in particular, the lyrics. You'll want the lyrics to reflect a real passion and intensity that brings out an emotional response. When you believe in the lyrics, they take on a whole new life that will help elevate the entire song.

Listen to Your Passions

Successful songwriters have an ability to tap into their passions, which then translate into good songwriting material. This is because the really good songs are the ones that relate to the emotion, drive, and interest of the songwriter. There are many different things that people are passionate about: love, money, family, and more. Some songs revolve around the loss of youth or days gone by, while others look forward into the future. Whatever fuels your passions should be the source of your songwriting.

Write Down Ideas Immediately

When you think of a great lyric or song idea, write it down on the spot and don't try to put it off. Carry a pad and pen or pencil with you, so when an idea pops into your head, you can put it straight to paper. In this manner, you can retain more of your lyric ideas and create more songs.

Take a Walk

Unfortunately, song ideas generally do not come from the ether as you sit in your comfortable chair. For the most part, they have to be inspired during some activity. One good way to help stir up some song ideas is by taking a walk in the country. A good hike in the fresh air will help the blood flow to your brain, which in turn, helps bring out more inspiration. In fact, getting out of the house and doing any number of healthy activities is a great way to stir the imagination and bring out great song ideas. So, whether you go for a walk, ride a bike, or take your travels to other parts of the world, your inspiration is out there.

Turn the Bad into the Good

For whatever reason, more people will remember the bad experiences in their lives over the good, even if they do not talk about them as much. The good news is that the bad experiences make for great songwriting material, as some of the most unforgettable songs have been about experiences that didn't quite go the way the songwriter wanted. As inspirational works, you can tap into your bad experiences in life and turn them into songs that do not have to be sad. In fact, they can be funny and even uplifting.

Work With Others

Sometimes, the best way to make a song is to find someone else to collaborate. You don't have to go any further than *Paul McCartney* and *John Lennon* to see what a collaborative effort means to creating songs. And while your songs may not become as popular as *The Beatles'*, you can still get a great deal of inspiration and joy from working with others while collaborating on songs. Quite often, collaboration is one person coming up with song ideas, while the other makes a few changes or edits to improve the overall effect.

Try Reading

By taking the time to read newspaper headlines, stories, magazines, blogs, and many different text sources, you can come up with great inspiration for your songs. Not only will you be provided with good song material, you will also expand your vocabulary, which you can use when writing lyrics. Reading should be part of your everyday activities.

Be Random

One of the best ways to choose song lyrics is by coming up with a few sayings or sentences along with your friends and pulling them out of a hat. You can even write just a word or two on each note and then pull two or three to make a sentence or simply an idea. Try singing the lyrics that you pull out of the hat, and if they work, you can try to put them into a song. It may sound really random at first, but when you think about how many great songs have lyrics that seem random, such as *"Burning Down the House"* by the *Talking Heads*, this method can really work.

Know When to Stop

There are times when you can push yourself too hard in trying to write a song, so that is when you need to take a break. Remember that songwriting is not like factory work, in that putting in more time does not mean you can write better songs. In fact, many great songs were written in just a few minutes. It is how you use the time that really counts. So, take a break and don't push yourself too hard in your songwriting efforts.

Conclusion

Songwriting should be **fun and entertaining,** so there should be no rules in composing new songs complete with lyrics and melody. First, keep in mind that you do not need to make a perfect song in one trial. You can write lyrics as many times as you can. Explore, internalize, and think deeply.

When creating melody, chords, rhythm etc., do not be afraid to **experiment on new sounds and techniques.** Do not be fixated on one style, and it is not even a requirement to make songs under one specific genre or music category. Try to incorporate other sounds and beats into your composition.

If you are wondering about the topic of a song that you should write, always remember that you are **free to make songs about anything.** But if you really want to use common themes, like love, break-up, marriage, hatred, etc. then do it in a better way. Avoid copying lines and thoughts from other songs; say it with a twist and make your song sound fresh and different from others.

Creating simple songs does not hurt. Some people prefer easy to sing and memorize types of songs. So why do you have to make them complicated? Simple tunes and lyrics do not mean poor quality or lack of talent in songwriting; sometimes, it is just good enough to reach the target audience and listeners.

SONGWRITING

Do not be afraid or intimidated. Ask some friends, family members, music enthusiasts, or fellow musicians to listen to your songs and ask for their opinions and suggestions and be open to criticism. It is one of the most effective tools to know if you are successful with your original composition. The best way to measure your composition is to have it listened to and rated by people of different ages, genders, professions, and music preferences.

Keep writing and never give up!

"Clear your mind of can't." -Samuel Johnson

If you want to get more tips on songwriting and my FREE report, 15 Tips to Overcome Songwriter's Block, you can subscribe to my newsletter at www.YourSongWriting.com

Finally, if you enjoyed this book, please take the time to share your thoughts and post a review on Amazon. It would be greatly appreciated!

HOW TO START A SONG

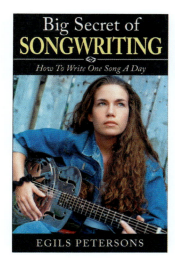

I also suggest my first book at Amazon: BIG SECRET OF SONGWRITING: How To Write One Song a Day

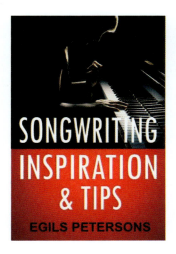

And my third book at Amazon: SONGWRITING INSPIRATION AND TIPS

God bless you!

Egils Petersons

Printed in Great Britain
by Amazon